MOTIVATED BY LOVE
Study Companion and Journal Included

Vera LeRay Warner

P.O. Box 236552 Cocoa, FL 32923

Warner, Vera LeRay Motivated by Love

ISBN: 978-0-9713072-6-1

Amplified Bible (AMP)

International Version (NIV) and New International Version UK (NIV-UK)

New King James Version (NKJV)

New Living Translation (NLT)

Message

Complete Jewish Bible

J. B. Phillips New Testament (PHILLIPS)

DEDICATION

Glynnis, Norma, Samoa, Shannon, Gillian and Rochelle
"The Sisters"

CONTENTS

ACKNOWLEDGEMENTS

First and foremost, I give all glory and honor to God, my Father, the Creator of the universe who so loves me that I could shout it from the roof tops!

To my husband and my best friend, who still makes me laugh after all these years. What a gift you are to me; so loving, patient and kind! I love you so much.

Much love to our children Nicolle and Michael Jr. I read somewhere recently that the greatest blessing is togetherness. Thanks for your sacrifice throughout the years. Mommy loves you more than you could possibly understand! We are finally on the same continent and it is fantastic!

To all our grandchildren: Mikal, Mya, Khalil, Myles, J.D., Dejón, Eric, Kason, Roman and Karman. You guys come from a rich family heritage and we are watching your lives for the continuance of the blessings!

To Yolanda, my sister and my friend. Once again your proofing skills challenge me to want to do the next work better than the last. Your gifting is a blessing to the body of Christ!

To Dr. Andy and my dearest prayer partner, Gabi, thank you for all the loving hours you put into translating the books into the German language. What a gift you are to the body of Christ and I am so grateful for you both!

To Marilyn Joyce, my longtime friend, author and sounding board. Your writing is a blessing and your advice is invaluable! Thank you, thank you, and thank you.

And finally to the Ministry Team of In His Image: Women of Excellence Ministries International. Oh, how blessed I am to have you guys in my life. Your prayers and support astound me. Love is the glue that has kept us together all these years and I am so glad that it continues to bond us!

PREFACE

We were created to be responders. We react either favorably or unfavorably to influences whether internally or externally. We can be motivated by what influences us the most.

The completion of the third book in the In His Image: Women of Excellence Certified Bible Study series was done. We had just released it a few months ago and had at least two book signings under our belts. I was looking forward to sitting on my literary laurels, not intending to write again for some time. I was minding my own business when I heard my Lord say to me, "Motivated by Love." His appeal to me was a lot different this time. There was no flurry of ideas that began to flow just the title of the book. And here I am 2 weeks later with pen in hand, praying for revelation!

We know that God is love and we understand that everything that we do for the Kingdom is supposed to be done as we are motivated by His love for us and our love for Him. Yet, when it comes to understanding His love; we might find ourselves always discovering that there is so much more to learn and embrace.

In the first book, *Embracing the Love of the Father*, we learned to embrace the Father's love as we went on the journey of discovering His love for us.

In the second book, *Cultivate My Heart*, we allowed His love to transform our hearts and in the process shaping our character to become more fruitful.

In the latest release, *The Making*, we went deeper into character building and now with *Motivated by Love* we will examine our works. The question being asked and answered will be, "Are my works truly motivated by my love for the Father?"

STUDY COMPANION AND JOURNAL INCLUDED

The Motivated by Love study companion and journal has been incorporated in this book. The study companion has been designed to assist the reader in discovering the reason why he or she do what they do for the kingdom of God.

The study companion can be used either in a small group setting or by an individual during personal devotional and or study time. It can be readily adapted for both.

Each chapter is followed by a study question section followed by Love Letters from the Father. This section is to write those things to reflect upon that are heard during quiet times of meditation while reflecting upon what has been gleaned.

If you are a leader in a small group setting I suggest that you do more extensive study to be able to supply more information than is given. It will make for livelier discussions when going through the question and answer section.

Before you begin:

♥ Pray that God would give you fresh revelation and show you ways to apply what you will learn in a very practical manner.

During the Course of the Study:

♥ Read the passage of scripture suggested more than once to get a clearer understanding of what is being conveyed.
♥ During the course of your studying write down your answers as it will aid in memory retention.
♥ Don't forget the importance of the journaling section. If you really desire Him to, God will speak to your heart deeply and personal. Write down what He speaks to your heart to be able to revisit it at a later date.

INTRODUCTION

It would be a good thing if we could say with confidence that, "Everything that I do is **motivated** by my love for God." Motivation is defined as the driving force by which we do a thing. It is that internal force that produces you to act. And it would be wise to remember that motivation always has a goal in mind. The reality is that everything that we do is not motivated by our love for God. God is love, and He loves us so much. So much so that he created us with the freedom to choose. We choose to love or not to love.

If love is the most powerful force on the planet; what do you think would happen if it was allowed to be unleashed to its fullest? I dare say that many wars would cease, lots of divorces would be virtually non-existent, many abortions would not happen and the list goes on. Notice that I did not say that none of them would be non-existent. The sad fact is that some would still choose to hate rather than love.

This study is going to be quite challenging. It will cause you to re-examine your motive for just about everything that you do for the Kingdom of God. It will prove to be quite a humbling experience, if you decide to become transparent and genuine and real. The children's book, The Velveteen Rabbit explains it this way, "Real isn't how you are made,' said the Skin Horse. 'It's a thing that happens to you. When a child loves you for a long, long time, not just to play with, but REALLY loves you, then you become Real. "Does it hurt?' asked the Rabbit. 'Sometimes,' said the Skin Horse, for he was always truthful. 'When you are Real you don't mind being hurt.' 'Does it happen all at once, like being wound up,' he asked, 'or bit by bit?' 'It doesn't happen all at once,' said the Skin Horse. 'You become. It takes a long time. That's why it doesn't happen often to people who break easily, or have sharp edges, or who have to be carefully kept. Generally, by the time you are Real, most of your hair has been loved off, and your eyes drop out and you get loose in the joints and very shabby. But these things don't matter at all, because once you are Real you can't be ugly, except to people who don't understand." — Margery Williams, *The Velveteen Rabbit*

Are you ready to be made "Real"? Are you ready to become more transparent than you have ever been in your life? Are you ready to allow God to unleash his love in you and through you so that you can truly be effective for Kingdom work? If you are then you will not be sorry for embarking on this journey though the next chapters and beyond.

Read on!!!

CHAPTER ONE

Unconditional Love Is **He**

And we have known and believed the love that God has for us. **God is love**,
and he who abides in love abides in God, and God in him.
1 John 4:16 New King James Version

While sitting here, attempting to write about the love of God, what comes to my mind is most unusual. I see a picture in my mind of an iceberg. I know what it is and that it exists. I can see the tip of it protruding out of the water; however, that is not the entire iceberg. In fact, the greatest part cannot be measured by its tip that is seen. The tip only makes up about 10% of its total mass. The greatest part of its mass is that which is under the water; the part that is unseen.

The Apostle Paul, in Ephesians the third chapter, explains to the saints in Ephesus the mystery surrounding the plan of God in that the Gentiles would be equal heirs of the Kingdom. At the end of the chapter he prays for them and in his prayer he said, *"When I think of the greatness of this great plan I fall on my knees before God the Father (from whom all fatherhood, earthly or heavenly, derives its name), and I pray that out of the glorious richness of his resources he will enable you to know the strength of the spirit's inner re-enforcement—that Christ may actually live in your hearts by your faith. And I pray that you, firmly fixed in love yourselves, may be able to grasp (with all Christians)* **how wide and deep and long and high is the love of Christ—and to know for yourselves that love so far beyond our comprehension**. *May you be filled through all your being with God himself!*[1]To try and explain just how wide and deep and long is the love of God would be a monumental task! It could take a person an entire life time of surrender and service, and he or she could write a 1000 books and still not even come close to a complete understanding of the unconditional love of God. Yet God gives us four measureable, somewhat

---

[1] Ephesians 3: 14-19 The New Testament in Modern English by J.B Phillips copyright © 1960, 1972 J. B. Phillips. Administered by The Archbishops' Council of the Church of England.

comprehensible types of love that helps us relate to him and others; Agape, Phileo, Eros and Storge.

These four Greek words for love: A*gape, Phileo, Eros and Storge* is a precursor to knowing God, and how He desires to know us, and as a result, us properly relating to one another. Eros is erotic love; a sensual love between a husband and a wife. The word does not directly appear in the Bible, but is portrayed in the Song of Solomon. Phileo is brotherly love, it is benevolent and it is kind.[2] Storge is the love-bond in the family. It is the love of the mother, father, sisters and brothers towards each other.[3] And then there is agape. Agape is selfless and sacrificial love. Agape is the very nature of God. Agape is unconditional love!

In explaining agape let's examine what it means to be *sacrificial and having little or no concern for oneself (being selfless)*. Sacrificial and being selfless are two concepts that describe the Old Testament scenario of Abraham taking his son Isaac, in response to God's request, to the region of Moriah with the intent of offering him up to God as a burnt offering. *Now it came to pass after these things that God tested Abraham, and said to him, "Abraham!" And he said, "Here I am." Then He said, "Take now your son, your only son Isaac, **whom you love**, and go to the land of Moriah, and offer him there as a burnt offering on one of the mountains of which I shall tell you."[4]* Depending upon which translation is used it is the first time that the word love is used. God told Abraham to take his only son. He also had another son, Ishmael, but here God referred to Isaac as Abraham's only son. Ishmael had, previous to this time, been cast out by Abraham; therefore, Isaac was the son who would receive his father's inheritance. (Interesting… what do you think would have happened if Ishmael would have stayed in the camp? Ishmael was not the promised son and would in no way had received the inheritance due Isaac.) He was the son of promise. Isaac's very name meant laughter, and here God was asking him to do something that would be a source of unimaginable grief. This was no laughing matter! He told him to offer his only son, the son whom he had waited so long for, the son that brought him so much joy: as a burnt offering. In order to understand the actions of Abraham let's explore what the burnt offering meant to him during this time. This was way before the regulations for the burnt offering were stipulated in the Book of Leviticus. We have to go back to Noah in Genesis

---

[2] Romans 12:10
[3] Exodus 20:12
[4] Genesis 22: 1-2 NKJV

chapter eight. The flood had occurred, and after being shut up in the ark along with his family and all the animals; the Lord caused a wind to blow, and the flood water began to recede. Little by little the water dried up until the ground became dry. Finally, God told Noah that it was alright to leave the ark, and he did, along with his family and all the animals. The first thing that Noah did was to build an altar to the Lord and offer up to him a burnt offering. The offering was received by God as a sweet fragrance, and it was then that God made a **covenant** promise that He would not destroy every living thing using a flood ever again.[5] So it could be said that Abraham viewed the burnt offering as a means of not being the object of the wrath of God, but instead acquiring and keeping His favor. The Israelites viewed this as a reminder that God was a **covenant** keeping God. Then if we go over to the New Testament it tells us, concerning Abraham, that he was absolutely assured that what God had promised him, he would perform![6] Abraham reasoned that if he did offer his son up as a burnt offering that God would raise him from the dead.[7] What faith! Up to this time it is not recorded that God had raised anyone from the dead! How could Abraham even assume this? Abraham passed the test set before him in that he did not hold back that one whom he loved so much. He proved to be selfless, and was willing to sacrifice his own happiness to be obedient to God. And God, in his love for Abraham and in his faithfulness to keep his word; provided a substitute for Isaac; proving to him that he was the **covenant** keeping God who loved unconditionally. I wonder if Abraham breathed a sigh of relief or just walked away in confidence or did he do both?

Okay so today we, western minded Christians, can look back on this episode between God, Abraham, and Isaac and see the foreshadowing of the ultimate picture of the unconditional/agape love of God for mankind. God gave his only begotten Son as the ultimate sacrifice for mankind as the propitiation for sin.[8] Christ is the perfect example of agape. Christ is the example of the unconditional love of the Father. Unconditional love says, "I love you without limitations. You do not have to do one thing to earn it. There are no strings attached." Unconditional love accepts and approves in spite of all that has been committed to warrant otherwise. Unconditional love loves you even if you do not reciprocate that love. Unconditional love is He!

---

[5] Genesis 8: 20-22
[6] Romans 4: 19-21
[7] Hebrews 11:19
[8] John 3:16

Christ left his heavenly home, was born of a virgin, lived as a mere mortal, endured shame and humiliation and scouring and death to save God's creation, hell bent on destruction. Humankind deserved nothing but the hell that was originally created for Satan and his angels. But God in his mercy and grace sent his Son Jesus to be sacrificed on the cross of Calvary, He died and He rose on the third day, so that we could be reconciled back to the Father. Now that is the ultimate example of unconditional love.

There is another account in scripture that I would like us to examine when referring to agape love. It is the story of the Prodigal Son. It is an example of patience, forgiveness, and restoration. As the account goes; there was a man who had two sons, and the younger son went to his father, and requested his inheritance. Not regarding the fact that an inheritance was not usually passed on to the heirs until after the death of the father. The father divided the inheritance between his two sons. The younger, not soon after left his father's house, squandered all that had been given to him. I cannot even begin to imagine the heart break of this father over the actions of his baby boy. There was a famine and the prodigal (prodigal describes one who is given to wasteful luxury or extravagance)[9] found himself hurting and hungry. At this point he would do whatever it took to survive. His circumstances brought him to his senses, and he decided to humble himself and go back home to his father, whereby with just the right apology he perhaps thought that he just might convince his dad to take him on as a hired hand. That would at least keep his belly full. So, he made his way back home, and while he was still afar off his father sees his foolish, reckless son, and he began to run towards him. In the culture at this time; older men did not run as it was a sign of humiliation. Matt Williams states in his article on the Prodigal Son, "In the first century, however, a Middle Eastern man never — ever — ran. If he were to run, he would have to hitch up his tunic so he would not trip. If he did this, it would show his bare legs. In that culture, it was humiliating and shameful for a man to show his bare legs."[10] There is also the Jewish custom during that time to consider. Kenneth Bailey, author of _The Cross & the Prodigal_, explains that if a Jewish son lost his inheritance among Gentiles, and then returned home, the community would perform a ceremony, called the _kezazah_. They would break a large pot in front of him and yell, "You are now cut off from your people!" The community would totally reject him. Could it be that the

---

[9] www.dictionary.search.yahoo.com

[10] Matt Williams, Talbot School of Theology https://magazine.biola.edu/article10-summer/the-prodigal-sons-father-shouldnt-have-run/

father risked being humiliated himself to save his son from the humiliation of being rejected and ridiculed by the entire community? As the prodigal began to repent and apologize, it was as if his father did not even hear it as he began to call the servants to make a celebration feast. They brought clean clothes and dressed him. He was given the best robe-his return in humility and shame was replaced with dignity and honor. The family signet ring was placed on his finger. His identity was reaffirmed, along with the authority he possessed as a true son. They placed sandals on his feet. During that time slaves did not wear shoes. The son was willing to become a slave or servant in the house of his father. But, the father affirmed that he was a son and not a slave. The one who was lost, and most had probably given up on him ever returning, was found and had come back home. All that his son deserved was to suffer the consequences of his actions. Privileges are always forfeited because of sin. But, that father never gave up on him. He patiently waited for him to return.[11] The father loved his son and apparently his love never changed for him, in spite of that son choosing money over what really mattered. The father had forgiven his son before he even uttered his, perhaps, pre-rehearsed apology. What a celebration of unconditional love!

I have done the best I could to attempt to explain agape. But, the truth is that all that I have written thus far does not even come close to the complete revelation of the Father's love towards us. On a personal level there are times that my heart so longs to understand just how much He loves me that I just weep in His presence!

My son sent me a video of he and his son. His son was fast asleep lying with his head on his chest. That baby (his son) was soundly asleep with not a care in the world. He drifted off to sleep listening to the rhythm of his father's beating heart. Oh, that I would listen for and hear the rhythmic beat of the Father's heart. I would drift into a state of trust and peace and joy and rest knowing that I am safe in His arms. *See what great love the Father has lavished on us, that we should be called children of God! And that is what we are! The reason the world does not know us is that it did not know him.*[12] God has lavished His love upon us. The origin of the word lavish according to Merriam Webster is from the middle French; lavasse, lavache and it means as in a downpour of rain.[13] Pour it on Lord! Let your love come upon us like rain! Drench us in your love!

---

[11] Luke 15:11-32
[12] 1 John 3:1
[13] www.merriam-webster.com

5

STUDY QUESTIONS

1. Explain how knowledge of the unconditional love of God can be described in relation to an iceberg.

_____

_____

_____

_____

_____

_____

_____

_____

_____

_____

2. In appreciation to God for the mystery that was revealed to him, the Apostle Paul prayed a prayer for the saints in Ephesus 3: 14-19. Please explain, in your own words, verses 16-19.

_____

_____

_____

_____

_____

_____

_____

_____

_____

_____

_____

3. Look up the following word in a Greek lexicon and write down its definition and as many scripture references where the word is used or implied in the word of God.

Agape

_____

_____

_____

_____

_____

_____

_____

_____

_____

_____

_____

_____

_____

Read Genesis 12, 13, 15, 16, 17, 18:1-16, 21:1-19, 22:1-19 before answering the following questions.

4. Explain the statement, "Agape is the very nature of God."

_____

_____

_____

_____

_____

_____

_____

_____

_____

_____

_____

_____

5. What was the covenant promise that God made to Abraham?

_____

_____

_____

_____

_____

_____

_____

_____

_____

_____

_____

_____

_____

_____

_____

_____

6. How much confidence do you think Abraham had in God and why?

_____

_____

_____

_____

_____

_____

_____

_____

_____

_____

_____

_____

_____

_____

_____

_____

7. Now it is time for an honest moment. Do you feel that you have enough confidence in the unconditional love of God that if He asked you to give up one of your children that you could?

_____

_____

_____

_____

_____

_____

_____

_____

8. Explain how agape love can be described as both selfless and sacrificial.

_____

_____

_____

_____

_____

_____

_____

_____

9. What does prodigal mean?

_____

_____

_____

_____

_____

_____

_____

10. When this father consented to his son's demand by giving him his inheritance and did not stand in the way of his son's leaving what does this tell you about the father's love for his son?

_____

_____

_____

_____

_____

_____

_____

_____

_____

_____

_____

11. Some time had passed and we are not told how long before the son returned home. What type of impact do you think the father's reaction to his son's return had upon the following?

Family

_____

_____

_____

_____

_____

_____

_____

Community

_____

_____

_____

_____

_____

_____

_____

_____

12. Can you think of any prodigals who are away from God? If so write their names down below and pray for their return.

_____

_____

_____

_____

_____

_____

_____

_____

_____

_____

13. What is the greatest display of unconditional love that you, personally, have witnessed in your life up to now?

_____

_____

_____

_____

_____

_____

_____

_____

_____

_____

14. Take some time and watch the movie, "Passion of the Christ" and afterwards write below ways that it portrayed the love of the Father.

_____

_____

_____

_____

_____

_____

_____

_____

_____

_____

_____

_____

_____

_____

_____

_____

_____

_____

_____

_____

15. Now write a word of thanks to God for His love for you.

_____

_____

_____

_____

_____

_____

_____

_____

_____

_____

_____

_____

LOVE NOTES FROM THE FATHER

CHAPTER TWO
Our Response to Perfect Love

And you shall love the Lord your God [a] out of and with your whole heart and out of and with all your soul (your life) and out of and with all your mind (with your faculty of thought and your moral understanding) and out of and with all your strength. This is the first and principal commandment. The second is like it and is this, You shall love your neighbor as yourself. There is no other commandment greater than these.
Mark 12:30-31 Amplified Bible, Classic Edition (AMPC)

In the last chapter I discussed God's unconditional love towards us. Now I will discuss our love towards Him. There is a popular phrase, "It is not so much what you say, but what you do that makes the difference." I can say that I love God all day long, but the proof of it is how I live my life for Him! Ultimately my love for Him should be demonstrated by my obedience to Him!

In Mark the twelfth chapter one of the scribes came to Jesus after hearing Him reasoning with the Sadducees and asked Him, "Which is the first commandment of all?" And, it is in His answer to him that we discern four ways that we are to respond to the love that God has for us. We are to love God with all or with our whole heart. We are to love God with all our soul. We are to love God with all our mind. We are to love God with all of our strength. Now what exactly does this look like? After reading Mark 12: 30-31 we can also see three categories of love; God's love toward us, our love towards God, and our love towards others. In my attempt to examine how they correlate I believe that we can go back to the book of Exodus, when God gave Moses the Ten Commandments, to give us a clearer understanding. I just love revelation. The Holy Spirit is so awesome in speaking to our hearts, especially when there is something that we do not quite understand. The first four of the Ten Commandments dealt with their relationship with God, and the last six dealt with their relationship with people.[14] Now

---

[14] Exodus 20:1-17

let's put the first four commandments and the four ways we are to love God side by side and see how they possibly correlate.

♥ Commandment 1 – *You shall have no other gods before me.*
Love principle 1- *You shall love the Lord your God out of and with your whole heart...*

You shall have **no other gods**... A god (small g) is anything that can become an object of worship. It is anything or anyone that we deem worthy of our love, devotion, adoration and affection. It is an idol. An idol is defined as an image used as an object of worship. It is a false god. It is one that is adored, often blindly or excessively.[15]

You "shall love" denotes purpose. It is a verbal noun (infinitive) and it means to aim to, to pursue, determined to do a thing.[16] We are to have a fierce determination to love the Lord. Our love for Him should cause us to pursue Him with everything in us.

You shall love the Lord...with your **whole heart**. I believe that God intends to be the only one that we worship. Our love for Him is to be from a heart that is so full of devotion and adoration and affection for Him that there is not room for idolatry. We are to love Him with our whole heart. Our affections for Him are not to be divided. We are not to be hypocritical in our love for Him. Our love for Him is to be absolutely genuine. It is to come from a place of purity that can only come from Him. He loved us first so that we could love. There are times when I am in His presence during times of worship that my heart is so full that it literally feels as if it could burst. I have very few words at times like these. Most times all I can do is weep. How a person can say that they love the Lord and not allow their emotions to engage is beyond me. To love with the whole heart involves engagement. To engage means to catch and keep fixed. It means to take part in and to occupy the attention. God created us with these emotions and when we allow ourselves to become so fixed upon the Lord and giving Him our undivided attention our hearts are automatically engaged and something spiritual happens every time!

---

[15] www.frreedictionary .com
[16] Keyword Study Bible NASB/Hebrew-Greek, Spiros Zodthiates, Th. D AMG International/ www.freedictionary.com

♥ Commandment 2 – *You shall not make for yourself a carved image-any likeness of anything that is in heaven above or that is in the earth beneath, or that is in the water under the earth: you shall not bow down to them. For I, the Lord your God, am a jealous God...*
Love Principle 2 - *...and with all your soul (your life) ...*

A graven image or a carved image is something made by the hands of man created to be an object of worship. It is an idol. Worship is the expression of love, devotion, reverence, honor and adoration towards someone or something that would be considered sacred, divine or important.

We are created in the image of God. The triune Godhead is the Father, the Son and the Holy Spirit. Our physical/spiritual make-up is three parts.[17] We are spiritual beings that possess a soul and occupy a body. The soul is that spiritual part of us that is an expression of who we are. It is the totality of the life that we live. We are to worship God and Him only with our lives. If we ascribe our worship to anything else that thing becomes an idol. Whatever God has given us in this life we are not to love those things or people more than we love God. That includes the gifts that He has bestowed upon us, our natural talents, other human beings (whether parents, spouses, siblings or children), or our possessions!

♥ Commandment 3 – *You shall not take the Name of the Lord your God in vain, for the Lord will not hold him guiltless who takes His Name in vain.*
Love principle 3 - *...with all your mind (with your faculty of thought and your moral understanding) ...*

Traditionally, I have always believed that the emphasis as to the interpretation of this Scripture has been; that using God's name in vain was to use His Name while cussing or to frivolously use the name of Jesus while expressing frustration or disgust. But during my study time the teacher in me suspected that there was much more to understanding this commandment. In researching the English words in the original language I found that the verb "take" is nasa or nasah and it means to lift, carry, take, accept, to bring forth or to hold up. The word vain is the noun laš - šāw[18] and it means deceit, deception, false visions, falsehood. So then to use the

---

[17] 1 Thessalonians 5:23
[18] www.biblehub.com

Lord's Name in vain is to use His Name to deceive or in deception. It is to use His Name to make false affirmations. It is to use the Father's Name in ways that would cast doubt upon who He is or what He can do. God's Name is His character and His character is His Name. The Hebrew Name of God as revealed in the Tanakh is "YHWH". Jehovah has the absence of the vowels which leaves "four" letters. The Biblical number four has to do with God's creative power. On the fourth day of creation He created the sun, moon and stars. They were created to divide night from day and time…the days, years and seasons. The seasons being the division of appointed times. In this century, especially, we have known so many to deceitfully say that Jesus was coming back on a specific day and time. The prediction came and went without His return. [19]There are so many who "prophelie" saying, "Thus said the Lord" and it does not line up with the word of God. So many that say, "The Lord told me to tell you…" and they have no more been sent by the Lord than the man in the moon! God help us to truly not use your Name in vain! Help us not to misrepresent You; using Your Name in a deceitful way! To love God is to revere Him so much that we would think twice about using His name deceitfully in any way.

Then there are the covenant names of God. It was through His Covenant Names that He revealed His character to His people Israel. I wonder if by "frivolously" entering into covenant with God was in fact a way that the children of Israel took His Name in vain? I think that we would do well to remember that it is a serious thing to enter into a covenant relationship with the Father, and to not take that covenant relationship seriously, could actually be construed as taking His Name in vain. If I say that I love God and believe that He is Who He says that He is and will do what He says that He can do; then my life should reflect what I believe to be so. To love God is to enter into a covenant relationship with Him that is genuine and that we take seriously.

We are to love the Lord with all of our mind. It is in the mind that we reason, have knowledge, our memory and we imagine. Let's look at all four of these in relation to loving God. Greg Simas in his article "How to Love God with All Your mind states that, "We love God with the mind in four ways: reason, knowledge, memory and imagination."[20] Now let us

---

[19] Matthew 24:36

[20] www.gregsimas.or/how-to-love-god-with-all-your-mind

examine each one.

➢ REASON…To reason is to think, understand and form judgments by the process of logic or a particular way of thinking. *Come now, and let us reason together, says the Lord. Though your sins are like scarlet, they shall be as white as snow; though they are red like crimson, they shall be like wool. Isaiah 1:18.* I love God because He created me and breathed His love into me. I understand that. It makes good sense to me! And because I am His child I can ask Him anything (we can talk things over) and He gives me understanding. Sometimes I just ask Him, "Why?" And He somehow speaks to me in a way that reassures me that all (everything) is alright and I am at rest. It makes sense to me.

➢ KNOWLEDGE… *This is the agreement (testament, covenant) that I will set up and conclude with them after those days, says the Lord: I will imprint My laws upon their hearts, and I will inscribe them on their minds (on their inmost thoughts and understanding) …Hebrews 10:16 Amplified Bible* We have to saturate our minds with the word of God. The more we really get to know Him (He is the word); the more we will love Him and the more we love Him; the more we will obey Him!

➢ MEMORY… *I will recount the loving-kindnesses of the Lord and the praiseworthy deeds of the Lord, according to all that the Lord has bestowed on us, and the great goodness to the house of Israel, which He has granted them according to His mercy and according to the multitude of His loving-kindnesses. Isaiah 63:7 AMPBC* When we remember what God has done for us in the past and where He has brought us from, it will lead to gratitude and worship. It will lead to more love for God!

➢ IMAGINATION… *When I view and consider Your heavens, the work of Your fingers, the moon and the stars, which You have ordained and established…Psalm 8:3 AMPBC For My thoughts are not your thoughts, neither are your ways My ways, says the Lord. For as the heavens are higher than the earth, so are My ways higher than your ways and My thoughts than your thoughts. Isaiah 55:8-9 AMPBC* The imagination is considered the creative expression of the mind. It is the creative process within that helps us to think outside the perimeters of what is considered the norm. It is in the imagination that our dreams (what could be) are formulated. God lovingly gives us His dreams for us. Then begins the process of those dreams coming to pass as we obey Him and love Him even more. He astounds us as He helps us to explore possibilities that we would not have attempted had it not been for Him in our lives! Oh, how I love the Giver of dreams!

♥ Commandment 4…*Remember the Sabbath Day, to keep it holy.*
Love Principle 4… *and out of and with all your strength.*

The word Sabbath in the Hebrew is sabbat (verb) and it means to stop, to cease or to keep. The theological meaning is rooted in God's rest following the six days of creation.[21] The first time that the Sabbath is mentioned in the Bible is in Exodus the 16th chapter. *"This is what the LORD commanded: 'Tomorrow is to be a day of rest, a holy Sabbath to the LORD. So bake what you want to bake and boil what you want to boil. Save whatever is left and keep it until morning.'" So they saved it until morning, as Moses commanded, and it did not stink or get maggots in it. "Eat it today," Moses said, "because today is a Sabbath to the LORD. You will not find any of it on the ground today. Six days you are to gather it, but on the seventh day, the Sabbath, there will not be any." Nevertheless, some of the people went out on the seventh day to gather it, but they found none. Then the LORD said to Moses, "How long will you refuse to keep my commands and my instructions? Bear in mind that the LORD has given you the Sabbath; that is why on the sixth day he gives you bread for two days. Everyone is to stay where he is on the seventh day; no one is to go out." So the people rested on the seventh day."* Exodus 16: 23-30 NIV

In doing research on the Sabbath in order to gain a greater understanding of how keeping the Sabbath holy would correlate with loving the Lord with all of our strength; I was so overwhelmed that I had to pray and think and pray and ponder for a long time. I reasoned and reasoned and prayed and reasoned to the point that I had to step away from it and come back to it at a later time. It was just to-

---

[21] www.biblestudytools.com (Bakers Evangelical Dictionary of Biblical Theology)

day as I write this that the Lord reminded me that I was not to do a commentary on the Sabbath so it was okay to keep it as simple as possible.

God commanded the Sabbath to be a separated day in that for six days work was to be done and expected, but the seventh, separated-sacred day was a day whereby physical labor was not to be done. It was not just cessation from physical labor but a day of sacred assembly as far as the ceremonial law was concerned in the Old Testament.[22] In the New Testament the first time that the Sabbath is mentioned is found in *Matthew 12:1-8:*

About that time, Jesus was walking one day through some grain fields with his disciples. It was on the Sabbath, the Jewish day of worship, and his disciples were hungry; so they began breaking off heads of wheat and eating the grain. *[2] But some Pharisees saw them do it and protested, "Your disciples are breaking the law. They are harvesting on the Sabbath." [3] But Jesus said to them, "Haven't you ever read what King David did when he and his friends were hungry? [4] He went into the Temple and they ate the special bread permitted to the priests alone. That was breaking the law too. [5] And haven't you ever read in the law of Moses how the priests on duty in the Temple may work on the Sabbath? [6] And truly, one is here who is greater than the Temple! [7] But if you had known the meaning of this Scripture verse, 'I want you to be merciful more than I want your offerings,' you would not have condemned those who aren't guilty! [8] For I, the Messiah,* [a] *am master even of the Sabbath." (Living Bible)*

I do not believe that it is a coincidence that 2,000 years before there is also mentioned food and the Sabbath concerning the Hebrews.[23] Jesus stated that He was Lord of the Sabbath. In other words, He was and is the One who has all authority over the Sabbath. He could do anything He pleased with, and on the Sabbath! Why? Because He created it! Now did Jesus go to the synagogue on the Sabbath? Yes.[24] It was there that He preached and taught because the people honored the ceremonial Sabbath. They had ceased from all work and had assembled together for worship.

Now let's bring this all the way up into the 21st century. Now for those who do not follow the ceremonial law of the Old Testament; ceasing from all labor from sundown Friday until sundown Saturday, but choose instead to set aside some other day to cease from labor and to assemble for worship…I would like to rea-

---

[22] Leviticus 23:1- 24:1
[23] Exodus 16
[24] Luke 4: 6

son that because Jesus is the Lord (Master) over the Sabbath that it is in Him that we find our Sabbath rest! Let's look at Matthew 11: 28-30 *[28] Come to Me, all you who labor and are heavy laden, and I will give you rest. [29] Take My yoke upon you and learn from Me, for I am gentle and lowly in heart, and you will find rest for your souls. [30] For My yoke is easy and My burden is light."* It is in Him that we find continual rest as we learn to lay burdens down at His feet and to cast our cares upon Him. Jesus is the representation of the Sabbath! The love principle is to love the Lord our God...out of and with all your strength. So, could it be said that when we come to Jesus weary, from labor, and burdened (with the cares of this life) that He (the presentation of the Sabbath) gives us "True Sabbath Rest" and it is not so much having our focus on just the cessation of physical labor, but release from emotional and psychological stress as well? The "True Sabbath Rest" will serve to remind us of our dependency on Him for all things and that His rest is a gift from Him. To trust is to rest. We can trust that He will take care of everything that we cannot. To love Him with all of our strength is to lay all of our burdens at His feet and to cast all our cares upon Him and He in turn will give us that Sabbath rest! His yoke is easy and His burden is light!

STUDY QUESTIONS

1. What did Jesus say was the greatest or the first commandment?

_____

_____

_____

_____

_____

2. What are the four ways that we are to respond to the love that God has for us?

_____

_____

_____

_____

_____

3. What are the three categories of love?

_____

_____

_____

_____

_____

4. List the first four of the Ten Commandments.

_____

_____

_____

_____

_____

5. List them alongside each love principle.

_____

_____

_____

_____

_____

6. Explain the meaning of idolatry.

_____

_____

_____

_____

7. How can we, purposely, love God?

_____

_____

_____

_____

_____

8. What does it mean, for you personally, to love the Lord with your whole heart?

_____

_____

_____

_____

_____

9. What is a graven or carved image, and what do they have to do with worship?

_____

_____

_____

_____

_____

10. Describe how we are to worship the Lord.

_____

_____

_____

_____

11. Explain at least two ways that we can use the Lord's Name in vain.

_____

_____

_____

_____

_____

_____

_____

_____

12. Research at least two of the compound or covenant names of God and describe His revealed character in the names you choose. Do not forget to also list the passage of Scripture where the Name can be found.

_____

_____

_____

_____

_____

13. We are to love God with all of our mind. List the four things we do with our mind and explain each one in relation to loving God.

_____

_____

_____

_____

_____

_____

_____

_____

_____

_____

_____

_____

_____

_____

_____

_____

_____

14. Explain what it means to remember the Sabbath Day and to keep it holy, and explain what that has to do with loving God.

_____

_____

_____

_____

_____

_____

15. How much, can you say that you love the Lord?

_____

_____

_____

_____

_____

_____

LOVE NOTES FROM THE FATHER

CHAPTER THREE
Giving Love Away

*And you shall love the Lord your God [a] out of and with your whole heart and out of and with all your soul (your life) and out of and with all your mind (with your faculty of thought and your moral understanding) and out of and with all your strength. This is the first and principal commandment. The second is like it and is this, **you shall love your neighbor as yourself.** There is no other commandment greater than these.*
Mark 12:30-31 Amplified Bible, Classic Edition (AMPC)

In Chapters one and two we discussed; God's love for us and our love for God and now we approach our love toward others as the scripture commands us to love our neighbors as ourselves or I like to think of it as giving our love away! I have often times limited myself in thinking that my neighbor is simply the person who lives next door or in back of me or down the street from me. No doubt I am not the only one who does this. But, in getting to know the Father it does not take me long to realize that He expects more than what I think. After all His thoughts are much higher than my own.[25] In researching the definition of neighbor in the original Greek, here is what I found.

> **Strong's Definition:** Neuter of a derivative of πέλας pelas (*near*); (adverb) *close* by; as noun, a *neighbor*, that is, *fellow* (as man, countryman, Christian or friend): - near, neighbor. **Thayer's Definition:** a neighbour is a friend, any other person, and where two are concerned, the other (thy fellow man, thy neighbour), according to the Jews, any member of the Hebrew nation and commonwealth, according to Christ, any other man irrespective of nation or religion with whom we live or whom we chance to meet.[26]

So, considering all of the aforementioned; my neighbor is humankind! Humankind is all people of the human race! This can be a little hard to accept, because

---

[25] Isaiah 55:9
[26] www.studylight.org/lexicons/greek/gwview.cgi?n=4139

from the time we come into this world we are being programmed by our parents, other relatives, teachers, and society as a whole. It is being programmed into us who we are to love, who we are to hate, and we are sometimes given the reasons for it and sometimes not. Our motivation to choose to love certain people or not run the gamut from religion to race, gender, social status and the list can go on and on. And yet, God has commanded us to love our neighbor (humankind as much as we love ourselves). It makes sense if we consider that simply because mankind was created in the image of God that, that in itself would be enough to love His creation. But sad to say for most it is not. I remember one day I said something so unkind to my husband. I would have been crushed if he had said to me what I said to him. Needless to say, the Holy Spirit immediately convicted me. He reminded me that Mike was His man before He was my husband! I gained a new respect for my husband that day, and I always pray that I would see him in the same manner that the Father sees him. I want to always treat him as I want him to treat me. I pray constantly that the Father will teach me how to love my husband. After 36-years of togetherness and marriage; there are times when God will prompt me to do something that I have never done before to show Mike that I love him. Action is a companion of love. We cannot say that we truly love someone without showing them that love in some way. God is simply amazing!

As I write this chapter there are two people that come to mind. One is of this century and the other is from long ago. Let's start with the one from this century, Mother Teresa. Lately, I have found quotes and heard stories of this little Roman Catholic (now diseased) nun/missionary that have interested me. She served the sick, poor and disadvantaged of humanity all of her adult life. I will now list at least two quotes by her that really got me to thinking. "People are often unreasonable, irrational, and self-centered. Forgive them anyway. If you are kind, people may accuse you of selfish, ulterior motives. Be kind anyway. If you are successful, you will win some unfaithful friends and some genuine enemies. Succeed anyway. If you are honest and sincere people may deceive you. Be honest and sincere anyway. What you spend years creating, others could destroy overnight. Create anyway. If you find serenity and happiness, some may be jealous. Be happy anyway. The good you do today, will often be forgotten. Do good anyway. Give the best you have, and it will never be enough. Give your best anyway. You see, in the final analysis, it is between you and God. It was never between you and them anyway." — Mother Teresa "The greatest disease in the West today is not TB or leprosy; it is being unwanted, unloved, and uncared for. We can cure physical diseases with medicine, but the only cure for loneliness, despair, and hopelessness is *love*. There are many in the world that are dying for a piece of bread, but there are many more dying for a little love. The poverty in the West is a different kind of poverty -- it is not only a poverty of loneliness, but also of spirituality. There's a hunger for love, as there is a hunger for God." — Mother Teresa, A Simple Path: Mother Teresa[27] I believe that she was on to something. The people that Mother Teresa poured her life (love) into were the poorest of the poor. They were both male and female, young and old and most times were afflicted with incurable disease. Most of them were not of her faith and yet she saw them all as God's creation. Her life's work was a picture of *Matthew 25: 35-40* [35] *For I was hungry and you fed me; I was thirsty and you gave me water; I was a stranger and you invited me into your homes;* [36] *naked and you clothed me; sick and in prison, and you visited me.* [37] *"Then these righteous ones will reply, 'Sir, when did we ever see you hungry and feed you? Or thirsty and give you anything to drink?* [38] *Or a stranger, and help you? Or naked, and clothe you?* [39] *When did we ever see you sick or in prison, and visit you?* [40] *"And I, the King, will tell them, 'When you did it to these my brothers, you were doing it to me!' Living Bible*

How and when and whom we love is ultimately between us and God. He is the one who has commanded us to love our neighbors as ourselves. As Christians we are to be obedient to do what He expects of us.

The second person is the woman with the alabaster jar. It was during the time of the Passover celebration, and the Jewish officials were meeting to discuss the best way to take Jesus captive. In the meantime, Jesus and his disciples were having dinner at the home of Simon, the leper. Suddenly a woman entered the home carrying with her an alabaster jar of very expensive perfume. She proceeded to pour the perfume on Jesus as an act of anointing him. The anointing of Jesus in accordance with Jewish tradition was an act of hospitality, but in this case Jesus stated that she did it in preparation for His burial. I wonder if she knew why she was doing what she did before Jesus revealed it. I wonder if after He revealed it; did she really understand? Whether she understood it or not I see a picture of love in action that blows my mind! It did not even make sense to the disciples. As a matter of fact, the disciples criticized her actions.[28] To be obedient is to love and to love is to be obedient no matter the cost! Sometimes how God will have us to show His love to others just does not make sense!

---

[27] www.goodreads.com
[28] Luke 7: 36-50

My husband and I had just arrived in Germany and I was invited to speak at a woman's retreat in the United Kingdom. The place where the retreat was held was The Priory of Our Lady of Peace Turvey Abbey. It was run by nuns of a Roman Catholic community living according to the Rule of Saint Benedict and affiliated to the Olivetan family of Benedictines. On the last morning of the retreat all the ladies were gathered for communion and foot washing. As we were preparing for the foot washing; Sister Lucy who was the head nun came in to our gathering and approached Sister Robin who was the organizer of the retreat and told her that she would like to wash her feet on the behalf of their community. We were all stunned! Almost immediately we experienced the presence of the Lord. It was as if He opened a giant vat of love oil and just poured it on each of us! As the women began washing one another's feet and earnestly praying it was as if the atmosphere thickened, even more, with His presence. I did not realize it but I was about to be humbled to the very core of my being! You see I had never had a problem washing someone else's feet. But I had a problem with someone washing mine. As I sat there I said to the Lord, "Lord no one has washed my feet." No sooner were the words formulated in my mind; one of the ladies who had waist length hair (it was affixed in a bun on the top of her head) came to me with a bowl of water and knelt at my feet. All I could do was weep. I did not expect what happened next. As I closed my eyes in prayer I began to feel droplets of water on my feet. When I opened my eyes, it was her tears and she had taken her hair down and began to wipe my feet with her hair. Even as I type this I am tearing up as I cannot even adequately explain the love of the Father that I felt being poured into and released in my heart. On the one hand I wanted her to get as far away from me as possible. I felt so unworthy! And yet, on-the-other-hand, I just wept and wept; my heart being poured out to my Father through my tears never wanting the moment to end! I never asked her what prompted her to do what she did the way she did it. At that very moment I knew that she loved me as the Father loved me through her. She could have said no to the Father but she did not. I know that it was the Father's love being displayed through her actions.

You know there is such a disregard for human life and we know that it all started in the garden. It was Satan's attack against those whom God created in His image that got us in the trouble that we are in but it is our everyday choices that keep us there. I have been pondering the notion that my body is the lowest form of who I am and that it is the me on the inside that will make a difference in the lives of those whom God connects me to and those whom I come in contact with on a daily basis. God help me to love my neighbor (humankind) as myself. Now I have given one example from the bible, another from this century and one that was very personal concerning loving humankind as ourselves. And yet it still leaves me with so many questions. I guess the greatest question is, "How much do we love ourselves?" It stands to reason that if we do not love ourselves that we cannot and will not truly love anyone else. The truth is that if we have issues with loving ourselves; there will always be limitations in our love for others. There will be barriers, walls and road blocks that affect our relationships. One of the places to start when examining ourselves is to ask ourselves a few questions:

- ♥ Are we harder on ourselves than on others? Do we berate ourselves?
- ♥ Do we get angry with ourselves easily? Depression counts as self-anger!
- ♥ Are there things about ourselves that we dislike and can't accept?
- ♥ Are there things in our past that we just can't forgive ourselves for?
- ♥ How do we talk to ourselves when we have done something stupid?[29]

When we find ourselves with "self-love" issues we must absolutely know that it is God's will that we love ourselves. It was He who created us, and He did not make a mistake! We must come to understand that we have His acceptance just as we are and to honestly accept the fact that there are some things about us that will not change in this life. Recently I asked a group of ladies, "If you could change anything about yourselves right now what would it be?" One of the ladies said two things and the third thing she said was to be taller. I immediately told her that the first two were possible and likely because they were God's will for all our lives but the third one, well it isn't going to happen and she laughed. We all laughed because at that very moment we all realized that there are some things about ourselves that we just need to accept and keep it moving! To sum up "self-love" issues; we have a choice to either keep on believing the lies of the enemy or to believe the truth of who God says we are and what we can do through Him. [6] So he answered and said to me: *This is the word of the LORD to Zerubbabel: 'Not by might nor by power, but by My Spirit,' says the LORD of hosts. Zechariah 4:6 NKJV* God loves us and accepts us just as we are and yet He does not let us remain as we are. His will is to take us from glory to ever increasing glory and from faith to faith. [30] Here is how we love each other as ourselves....

---

[29] http://www.healingstreamsusa.org/overcome-low-self-worth-self-image-c18.html
[30] 2 Corinthians 3: 18 NASB

[31] Treat others as you want them to treat you. Luke 6: 31 Living Bible (TLB)

If I speak with human eloquence and angelic ecstasy but don't love, I'm nothing but the creaking of a rusty gate.[2] If I speak God's Word with power, revealing all his mysteries and making everything plain as day, and if I have faith that says to a mountain, "Jump," and it jumps, but I don't love, I'm nothing. [3-7] If I give everything I own to the poor and even go to the stake to be burned as a martyr, but I don't love, I've gotten nowhere. So, no matter what I say, what I believe, and what I do, I'm bankrupt without love.

Love never gives up.
Love cares more for others than for self.
Love doesn't want what it doesn't have.
Love doesn't strut,
Doesn't have a swelled head,
Doesn't force itself on others,
Isn't always "me first,"
Doesn't fly off the handle,
Doesn't keep score of the sins of others,
Doesn't revel when others grovel,
Takes pleasure in the flowering of truth,
Puts up with anything,
Trusts God always,
Always looks for the best,
Never looks back,
But keeps going to the end.

[8-10] Love never dies. Inspired speech will be over some day; praying in tongues will end; understanding will reach its limit. We know only a portion of the truth, and what we say about God is always incomplete. But when the Complete arrives, our incompletes will be canceled. [11] When I was an infant at my mother's breast, I gurgled and cooed like any infant. When I grew up, I left those infant ways for good. [12] We don't yet see things clearly. We're squinting in a fog, peering through a mist. But it won't be long before the weather clears and the sun shines bright! We'll see it all then, see it all as clearly as God sees us, knowing him directly just as he knows us! [13] But for right now, until that completeness, we have three things to do to lead us toward that consummation: Trust steadily in God, hope unswervingly, love extravagantly. And the best of the three is love.
1 Corinthians 13: 1- 13 <u>The Message</u> (MSG)

Lord teach us to truly love our neighbors as ourselves! Remember there is always action involved with loving others. We show love through respect (appreciation and consideration) which is shown through simple acts of kindness. Everybody just wants to be loved whether they realize it or not. Father, teach us how to give our love away!

STUDY QUESTIONS

1. Who is your neighbor?

_____

_____

_____

_____

_____

2. Why do you think God has commanded us to love our neighbors as ourselves?

_____

_____

_____

_____

_____

3. Characterize the people that Mother Teresa ministered to. What was so special about her ministry?

_____

_____

_____

_____

_____

...ow and whom we love is ultimately between us and

_____

_____

_____

_____

_____

_____

5. Read the account of the woman who anointed Jesus from all four Gospels: Matthew 26: 6-13, Mark 14: 3-9, Luke 7: 36-50 and John 12: 1-8. List all the similarities and differences using the who, what, when, where and how format.

_____

_____

_____

_____

_____

_____

_____

_____

_____

_____

_____

_____

_____

6. Write what you, personally, gleaned from the examination of the Scriptures.

_____

_____

_____

_____

_____

7. How do you witness disregard for human life on a daily basis?

_____

_____

_____

_____

8. What can you do to change this?

_____

_____

_____

_____

9. Do you love yourself? Give reasons for your response.

_____

_____

_____

_____

_____

10. If you could change anything about yourself, right now, what would it be and why?

_____

_____

_____

_____

_____

_____

11. Explain how we can love each other as ourselves. Use 1 Corinthians 13: 1-13 as your guide.

_____

_____

_____

_____

_____

_____

12. Now write out a prayer asking the Lord to teach you how to love.

_____

_____

_____

_____

_____

_____

_____

LOVE NOTES FROM THE FATHER

_____

_____

_____

_____

_____

_____

_____

_____

_____

_____

_____

_____

_____

_____

_____

_____

_____

_____

_____

CHAPTER FOUR
Lust of the Flesh

For all that is in the world—the lust of the flesh [craving for sensual gratification] and the lust of the eyes [greedy longings of the mind] and the pride of life [assurance in one's own resources or in the stability of earthly things]—these do not come from the Father but are from the world [itself].
1 John 2:16 Amplified Bible

We are not always motivated by our love for God. As a matter of fact, even as saints of God, there can be negative motivating factors in operation cleverly disguised in our service for Him. And it can all be traced back to the Garden of Eden. In Genesis chapter 3 when the serpent approached Eve she was tempted by the serpent in three areas of temptation; **the lust of the flesh**, **the lust of the eyes** and **the pride of life**. All sin can be categorized in at least one of these, therefore, all negative motivating factors can be found in at least one of these too.

So when the woman saw that the tree was good for food, that it was pleasant to the eyes, and a tree desirable to make one wise, she took of its fruit and ate. She also gave to her husband with her, and he ate.
Genesis 3:6 NKJV

- **Lust of the flesh**- Eve saw that the tree was good for food…
- **Lust of the eyes**-it was pleasant to her eyes…
- **Pride of Life**-She was told that it was desirable to make one wise…

All three were again present in the wilderness when Jesus was tempted by the enemy.

- **Lust of the flesh** - *Now when the tempter came to Him, he said, "If You are the Son of God, command that these stones become bread." Matthew 4:3*
- **Lust of the eyes** - *Then the devil took Him up into the holy city, set Him on the pinnacle of the temple and said to Him, "If You are the Son of God, throw Yourself down. For it is written: 'He shall give His angels charge over you,' and, 'In their hands they shall bear you up, Lest you dash your foot against a stone.'" Matthew 4:5-6*
- **Pride of life** - *Again, the devil took Him up on an exceedingly high mountain, and showed Him all the kingdoms of the world and their glory. Matthew 4:8*

In this chapter and the next two we will discuss all three in-depth. Now let's examine the "Lust of the Flesh".

Lust of the Flesh...

In order to understand what lust of the flesh is; we must first define what the Bible means by the flesh! The Greek word for flesh is sárks - (*sarks*) is generally negative, referring to making decisions (actions) *according to self* – i.e. done *apart from faith* (independent from *God's* in-working). What is "*of the flesh (carnal)*" by definition is displeasing to the Lord – even things that *seem* "respectable!" In short, *flesh* generally relates to *unaided human effort*, i.e. decisions (actions) that originate from self or are empowered by self. It is *carnal* ("of the *flesh*") and proceeds out of the *untouched* (*unchanged*) part of us – i.e. what is *not* transformed by God.[31] And giving in to the lust of the flesh can lead to the works of the flesh listed in *Galatians 5:19-21 NKJV*

Now the works of the flesh are evident, which are: adultery, fornication, uncleanness, lewdness, idolatry, sorcery, hatred, contentions, jealousies, outbursts of wrath, selfish ambitions, dissensions, heresies, envy, murders, drunkenness, revelries, and the like; of which I tell you beforehand, just as I also told you in time past, that those who practice such things will not inherit the kingdom of God.

---

[31] www.biblehub.com/greek/4561.htm

Susanna Wesley, mother to the great preachers and hymn writers John and Charles Wesley, described sin of the flesh this way: "Whatever weakens your reasoning, impairs the tenderness of your conscience, obscures your sense of God, or takes away your relish for spiritual things, in short – if anything increases the authority and the power of the flesh over the Spirit, that to you becomes sin however good it is in itself."[32] Ouch! To sum it up; lust of the flesh is the almost insatiable, over whelming desire or craving to do or act upon those things that gratify our unregenerate nature/flesh. It is further making decisions or actions without or independent of God's help.

The flesh can deceive even the most spiritually mature into getting its way if not careful. If you want to really know how powerful your flesh is…those carnal desires, try going on an extended fast! When the Lord began to teach me about fasting in the beginning of my walk with Him; I felt the need to go on a three day absolute fast. That meant that for three days I would not eat or drink anything at all, but would spend my time in prayer and fellowship with the Lord. This is what I committed to, and I was determined to see it through, because I wanted to hear from God. I needed direction. I just wanted to be with Him. The first day was a breeze. The second day I was so hungry I could have eaten the paint off of a barn, and to reward myself for making it through the first two days and having experienced the presence of the Lord like I had never before; I went before the Lord hoping that He would let me dishonor my commitment and stop the fast. I got down on the side of my bed in my most perfect position of prayer and honestly told the Lord how hungry I was. I waited intently upon Him to tell me, "Daughter you have abstained enough. The fast is over. You may now eat!" I waited and I waited. Then suddenly I heard the Father speak in that still small voice Deuteronomy 8:3. I had no idea what that verse of Scripture was so I got my Bible and looked it up. And there it was; my answer! *And he humbled thee, and suffered thee to hunger, and fed thee with manna, which thou knewest not, neither did thy fathers know; that he might make thee know that man doth not live by bread only, but by every word that proceedeth out of the mouth of the LORD doth man live.* I wanted to cry! I think that I did! Because that is not what I wanted to hear! Did it get better no! I could literally feel my flesh warring against the Spirit! I thought I was going to faint, no die! I learned that I have to feed my spirit to keep it strong. If not, the flesh will triumph into tricking me to do what it wants! I could have made a decision independent of God's help and just broken the fast. Thank God I did go to Him and I sought out His help! And

---

[32] www.goodreads.com/author/474367.Susanna_Wesley

in case you are wondering; I did finish the fast and God blessed me tremendously for my obedience. Now let's examine a husband and wife team who, unfortunately, had a problem with lush of the flesh and it cost them their lives!

In Acts the 4th chapter the church was in such unity of heart and mind that the believers who owned land and houses saw the needs of the fellow believers and decided to do something about it. They sold them and brought the money to the apostles. The apostles, in turn, distributed to the saints in accordance to the need. No doubt Ananias and his wife Sapphira witnessed the generosity and decided that it was something that they should also do. However, we find that no matter how good their actions seemed on the surface...The truth was that their decision to appear generous originated from that unregenerated part of them. It was actually rooted in human effort unaided by the Holy Spirit. Their decision empowered by self. The motive behind what they did would be exposed by the Holy Spirit and the judgment from God, for their act, would be death. Their yielding to the temptation of lust of the flesh caused them to have selfish ambition and selfish ambition (pretending to be something that they were not) led to lying and the lying led to death! It reminds me of *James 1:13-15[13] And remember, when someone wants to do wrong it is never God who is tempting him, for God never wants to do wrong and never tempts anyone else to do it. [14] Temptation is the pull of man's own evil thoughts and wishes. [15] These evil thoughts lead to evil actions and afterwards to the death penalty from God. Living Bible* The account of Ananias and Sapphira is an example for us all to seek God to honestly determine the motivation of our heart.

STUDY QUESTIONS

1. What are the three areas of temptation?

_____

_____

_____

_____

_____

2. Write the definition for lust of the flesh.

_____

_____

_____

_____

_____

3. How did Susanna Wesley describe sin and the flesh?

_____

_____

_____

_____

_____

4. Research and record as many Scriptures as you can find that reference carnality.

_____

_____

_____

_____

_____

5. Does carnality apply only to the unbeliever? Give a reason for your answer.

_____

_____

_____

_____

_____

Read Acts 5:1-11 using at least three different translations before answering the following questions.

6. Who was Ananias and Sapphira?

_____

_____

_____

_____

7. Do you believe that they were believers or unbelievers? Give the reason for your answer.

_____

_____

_____

_____

_____

8. Can you remember an incident when you believe that you were being led by lust of the flesh? What was the outcome of that incident?

_____

_____

_____

_____

_____

_____

_____

_____

_____

_____

_____

Read James 1:13-15 using as least three different translations of the Bible before answering the following questions.

9. When we are being tempted to do wrong; who is it that tempts us?

_____

_____

_____

_____

10. What is temptation?

_____

_____

_____

_____

11. What can temptation lead to?

_____

_____

_____

_____

12. How can we not give in to the lust of the flesh?

_____

_____

_____

_____

_____

13. Write out a prayer asking the Lord's help in this area.

_____

_____

_____

_____

_____

_____

LOVE NOTES FROM THE FATHER

_____

_____

_____

_____

_____

_____

_____

_____

_____

_____

_____

_____

_____

_____

_____

_____

_____

_____

_____

_____

CHAPTER FIVE

Lust of the Eyes

For all that is in the world—the lust of the flesh [craving for sensual grati-
fication] and the lust of the eyes [greedy longings of the mind] and the pri-
de of life [assurance in one's own resources or in the stability of earthly
things]—these do not come from the Father but are from the world [itself].
1 John 2:16 Amplified Bible

²² 'The eye is the lamp of the body.' So if you have a 'good eye' [that is, if
you are generous] your whole body will be full of light; ²³ but if you have
an 'evil eye' [if you are stingy] your whole body will be full of darkness. If,
then, the light in you is darkness, how great is that darkness! Matthew
6:22-23 Complete Jewish Bible (CJB)

When we speak of lust of the eyes; it is not necessarily the overwhelming desire
to please what the physical eye sees, but it is the overwhelming desire or craving
to satisfy the greedy cravings of the **soul** or **the mind**. Matthew 6:22-23 is
sandwiched right between verses 19-21 (laying up treasures in heaven) and
verse 24- not serving God and money. Now the question is, "What does money
have to do with having a good eye and a bad or evil eye, if the eye is the soul or
the mind?" We have already covered the mind in chapter two, but I feel that it is
necessary to dig a little deeper in studying the mind in relation to our soul.

Hebrews 4: 12 (NIV) ¹² For the word of God is alive and active. Sharper
than any double-edged sword, it penetrates even to dividing soul and spi-
rit, joints and marrow; it judges the thoughts and attitudes of the heart.

The soul is the mediator between the spirit and the body. It is our humanness.
It is where our mind is housed…the part of us that reasons, thinks, perceives,
and judges. It is our intellect or understanding. It is our sanity. It is our mental
condition. It is our soundness or unsoundness of mind. It is where we think

(reasoning and rationality), perceive (recognize, discern, understand), judge (we see, hear and decide or form an authoritative opinion). It is where our memories are stored and where our vocabulary is established/located. The soul is where our *will* is found. The *will* is the act or process of choosing to act or not to act. It is where we purpose or are determined to either do or not to do a thing-our decision making process. The soul is where our emotions are…something within us that causes a reaction. Our emotions are our feelings-our sensitivities (response to something that stimulates something on the inside of us) and susceptibilities (capacity for receiving mental or moral impressions, an image in the mind caused by something external to it). The soul also houses our self-consciousness or self-interest…our desires…process of all info based on our surroundings. This is probably the greatest enemy to the soul and will cause us to fail every time!

> [22] *'The eye is the lamp of the body.' So if you have a 'good eye' [that is, if you are generous] your whole body will be full of light;* [23] *but if you have an 'evil eye' [if you are stingy] your whole body will be full of darkness. If, then, the light in you is darkness, how great is that darkness!*
> *Matthew 6: 22-23 Complete Jewish Bible (CJB)*

The eye (Soul) is the lamp of the body. Lamps in the biblical days were so important. The lamp brought light to what was otherwise darkness. It was used to light the path in the dark so that the person could see where they were going. When we get saved it is our spirit man that is regenerated, and it is the soul man that has to be renewed on a daily basis.

> *For you were once darkness, but now you are light in the Lord. Live as children of light (for the fruit of the light consists in all goodness, righteousness and truth) and find out what pleases the Lord.* [33] *Since you have heard about Jesus and have learned the truth that comes from him, throw off your old sinful nature and your former way of life, which is corrupted by lust and deception. Instead, let the Spirit renew your thoughts and attitudes. Put on your new nature, created to be like God—truly righteous and holy.* [34]

---

[33] Ephesians 5: 8-10 CJB
[34] Ephesians 4: 22-24 NLT

We can choose to walk in darkness or light. We can choose to either be generous or stingy. It is an act of the will. To have a good eye means we choose to be generous or to walk in the light (in God's word). We willingly choose to be kind and generous. This is the character of the Father. In contrast we can choose to have a bad eye which means we choose to walk in darkness; unwilling to be kind and generous. Generosity does not always involve money. However, a couple of weeks ago the Lord began to minister to me concerning being motivated by money. The issue was not that I wanted to earn more, as this usually comes with promotion, but the issue was to not allow the accusation of money to become the motivating factor in the choices that I make; especially when it pertains to the things of God. The Apostle Paul told Timothy that true religion does bring great riches, but only to those who are content with what they have.[35] I take that to mean that when my motivating factor is not to crave for and chase after riches, riches will find me.

[19] "Do not store up for yourselves wealth here on earth, where moths and rust destroy, and burglars break in and steal. [20] Instead, store up for yourselves wealth in heaven, where neither moth nor rust destroys, and burglars do not break in or steal. [21] For where your wealth is, there your heart will be also. [22] 'The eye is the lamp of the body.' So if you have a 'good eye' [that is, if you are generous] your whole body will be full of light; [23] but if you have an 'evil eye' [if you are stingy] your whole body will be full of darkness. If, then, the light in you is darkness, how great is that darkness! [24] No one can be slave to two masters; for he will either hate the first and love the second, or scorn the second and be loyal to the first. You can't be a slave to both God and money. [25] "Therefore, I tell you, don't worry about your life — what you will eat or drink; or about your body — what you will wear. Isn't life more than food and the body more than clothing? [26] Look at the birds flying about! They neither plant nor harvest, nor do they gather food into barns; yet your heavenly Father feeds them. Aren't you worth more than they are? [27] Can any of you by worrying add a single hour to his life? [28] "And why be anxious about clothing? Think about the fields of wild irises, and how they grow. They neither work nor spin thread, [29] yet I tell you that not even Solomon in all his glory was clothed as beautifully as one of these. [30] If this is how God clothes grass in the field — which is here today and gone tomorrow, thrown in an oven — won't he much more clothe you? What little trust you have! [31] "So don't be anxious, asking, 'What will we eat?' 'What will we drink?' or 'How will we be clothed?' [32] For it is the pagans who set their

---

[35] 1 Timothy 6: 1-10 CJB

hearts on all these things. Your heavenly Father knows you need them all.
³³ But seek first his Kingdom and his righteousness, and all these things will
be given to you as well. ³⁴ Don't worry about tomorrow — tomorrow will
worry about itself! Today has enough tsuris) already!³⁶

Now let's examine the love of money.

For the love of money is a root of all evils; it is through this craving that some
have been led astray and have wandered from the faith and pierced themselves
through with many acute [mental] pangs.³⁷ Money is not evil, but the love of
money is. It kind of makes you wonder, if the love of money is the root of all
evil what kind of tree fruit does will it produce? We would often tell our children when they would ask for certain things that, "Money does not grow on
trees, and we cannot go out in the yard and just pick off a few bills to get you
what you want." But, sad to say, the love of money is a root that grows a tree
that produces some nasty tasting fruit. Let's take a very candid look at what this
might look like in accordance with scripture.

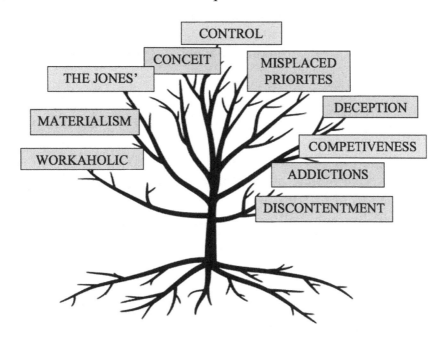

Love of Money: "Root of all evil"
1 Timothy 6: 4-9

---

³⁶ Matthew 6: 9-34 CJB
³⁷ 1 Timothy 6:10 Amplified Bible

Distasteful Fruit

- ➢ Addictions-strong and often harmful need to regularly have something, compulsive need for something that could become a habit.
- ➢ Competitiveness-compulsion to be as good or better or to have more than someone else.
- ➢ Conceit- has too much pride in your own goodness or works.
- ➢ Control-using manipulation to direct the behavior of someone to get what you want.
- ➢ Deception-making someone believe something that is not true, pretending to have something or to be somebody that you are not.
- ➢ Discontentment-not satisfied to the point where you would do anything to get more or to get ahead.
- ➢ Trying to be like the Jones'-coveting- strongly desiring what belongs to another.
- ➢ Materialism-thinking that places too much emphasis on material possessions.
- ➢ Misplaced priorities- what should be the most important things are now reduced to things of little or no importance.
- ➢ Workaholic- chooses to work compulsively at the expense of more important things.[38]

Oh how many people have sold their souls to become rich only to find their lives quite different from what they expected? There are many stories of those who have played the lottery, won, and received millions only to find themselves a few years later; broke, busted and disgusted! How many saints have given money to ministries or individuals motivated by a word of prophecy that they will become millionaires, and years down the road find themselves in debt up to their eyeballs. Could it be because they could not handle what God had already given them? Then they wonder why God has held back what He has promised. Perhaps they never considered that God had already given the million to them in all that they had received thus far, and they had simply squandered it by not being good stewards! God expects us to be generous and not stingy, but he also expects us to be good stewards of what He does give us!

---

[38] www.merriam-webster.com

Lust of the eyes can have us deceived into thinking that we are doing good by when we name it and claim it and blab it and grab it. It's mine all mine and you can't have any! I am a self-made man look at all that I have achieved. He must be lazy not to have come as far as I have. And the list goes on and on and on!

STUDY QUESTIONS

1. Finish the sentence...Lust of the eye is not necessarily the overwhelming desire to please what the physical eye sees but it is

_____

_____

_____

_____

_____

Before answering the following questions please read Matthew 6: 19-23 from both the Amplified and Complete Jewish Bible translations.

2. What does money have to do with having a good eye and a bad eye or evil eye in regard when the eye is referred to as the soul or mind?

_____

_____

_____

_____

_____

_____

_____

_____

3. Explain the soul being the lamp of the body. Draw a diagram to support your explanation.

_____

_____

_____

_____

_____

_____

_____

_____

4. Explain the difference between being generous and being stingy.

_____

_____

_____

_____

_____

Read 1 Timothy 6: 4-9 from at least three translations before answering the following questions.

5. Explain the love of money being the root of all evil.

_____

_____

_____

_____

_____

6. After examining the tree illustration, in what area or areas have you struggled? And remember you are not alone. We have all struggled in at least one of these at one time or another!

_____

_____

_____

_____

_____

7. How did you overcome or are you still struggling?

_____

_____

_____

_____

_____

8. Look up the following Scriptures and write them down: Joshua 7:21, Psalm 62: 10, Proverbs 15:27, Ecclesiastes 2: 19, Matthew 6:19 and Matthew 13:22.

_____

_____

_____

_____

_____

_____

_____

_____

_____

9. Now is the time to repent if you need to and to ask for the Lord's help. Write out what you are feeling in your heart right now in the form of a prayer.

_____

_____

_____

_____

_____

_____

_____

_____

_____

_____

_____

_____

_____

_____

_____

_____

_____

_____

_____

_____

_____

_____

LOVE NOTES FROM THE FATHER

_____

_____

_____

_____

_____

_____

_____

_____

_____

_____

_____

_____

_____

_____

_____

_____

_____

_____

CHAPTER SIX

Pride of Life

For all that is in the world—the lust of the flesh [craving for sensual grati-fication] and the lust of the eyes [greedy longings of the mind] and the pri-de of life [assurance in one's own resources or in the stability of earthly things]—these do not come from the Father but are from the world [itself].
1 John 2:16 Amplified Bible

...all the kingdoms of the world and their glory.[39] The Amplified Bible describes the pride of life as the assurance in one's own resources or in the stability of earthly things.[40] Now let's attempt to break this definition down to give us clearer understanding. One of the synonyms for assurance is self-confidence. Self-confidence is defined as assurance in your own abilities, power and personal judgment.[41] *Resource* is capability, ingenuity and initiative. It is also defined as economic wealth and a supply or source of aid.[42] So to put it all together; the pride of life can be self-confidence in your own abilities, power, personal judgment, capabilities, ingenuity, initiative, and wealth. Assurance is also defined as the stability of earthly things as well as presumptuous boldness.[43] This type of assurance will make you boast in your own accomplishments. And yet the Apostle Paul said in 2 Corinthians 11: 22-33[22:]

> *They are Hebrews? So am I! They are Israelites? So am I! They are descendants of Abraham? So am I!* [23] *Are they [ministering] servants of Christ (the Messiah)? I am talking like one beside himself, [but] I am more, with far more extensive and abundant labors, with far more imprisonments, [beaten] with countless stripes, and frequently [at the*

---

[39] Luke 4: 5b
[40] 1 John 2:16
[41] www.freedictionary.com
[42] www.freedictionary.com
[43] www.freedictionary.com

point of] death. [24] Five times I received from [the hands of] the Jews forty [lashes all] but one; [25] Three times I have been beaten with rods; once I was stoned. Three times I have been aboard a ship wrecked at sea; a [whole] night and a day I have spent [adrift] on the deep;[26] Many times on journeys, [exposed to] perils from rivers, perils from bandits, perils from [my own] nation, perils from the Gentiles, perils in the city, perils in the desert places, perils in the sea, perils from those posing as believers [but destitute of Christian knowledge and piety]; [27] In toil and hardship, watching often [through sleepless nights], in hunger and thirst, frequently driven to fasting by want, in cold and exposure and lack of clothing. [28] And besides those things that are without, there is the daily [inescapable pressure] of my care and anxiety for all the churches! [29] Who is weak, and I do not feel [his] weakness? Who is made to stumble and fall and have his faith hurt, and I am not on fire [with sorrow or indignation]? [30] If I must boast, I will boast of the things that [show] my infirmity [of the things by which I am made weak and contemptible in the eyes of my opponents]. [31] The God and Father of the Lord Jesus Christ knows, He Who is blessed and to be praised forevermore, that I do not lie. [32] In Damascus, the city governor acting under King Aretas guarded the city of Damascus [on purpose] to arrest me, [33] And I was [actually] let down in a [rope] basket or hamper through a window (a small door) in the wall, and I escaped through his fingers.

Boasting is a statement in which you express too much pride in yourself or in something you have, have done, or are connected to in some way.[44] Boasting or to boast is further defined as to glorify oneself in speech; to talk in a self-admiring way.[45] To boast means to speak with pride often excessive pride, usually about oneself or something related to oneself.[46] Paul had every reason to boast concerning the things that he had gone through. He said that if he must boast he would boast of the things that showed his weakness and not his strength. Man, what an example to follow!

When the devil took Jesus up to the highest peak and showed Him all the kingdoms and their glory and told him that all of it could be His... In my mind I see a king overlooking his kingdom, proud of what he had gained or accomplished in his own power and strength. But Jesus refused what the cross had not obtained

---

[44] www.merriam-webster.com

[45] www.freedictionary.com

[46] www.freedictionary.com

yet. It would be His blood and the cross that would declare Him King of kings! It was never our Lord's intention to boast nor to be puffed up with pride concerning the things of this world and neither should we.

Psalm 138:6 NKJV Though the Lord *is on high, yet He regards the lowly; but the proud He knows from afar.*

Proverbs 11:2 NKJV When pride comes, then comes shame; but with the humble is wisdom.

Proverbs 18:12 NKJV Before destruction the heart of a man is haughty, And before honor is humility.

When we are motivated by the pride of life we will have a tendency to put our trust in and have our total reliance upon earthy things. Many years ago after spending some time with the Lord; I had an open vision. As I was lying on my bed I saw tiny insects that looked like miniature moths flying in a circle over the head of the bed. I questioned, "Lord, what is this?" Matthew 6: 19-21 is what the Lord replied.

[19] Do not gather and heap up and store up for yourselves treasures on earth, where moth and rust and worm consume and destroy, and where thieves break through and steal. [20] But gather and heap up and store for yourselves treasures in heaven, where neither moth nor rust nor worm consume and destroy, and where thieves do not break through and steal; [21] For where your treasure is, there will your heart be also.[47]

Now let's examine humility, the very opposite of pride. Humility is the state of being humble. It is meekness or modesty in behavior, attitude, or spirit. It is the opposite of arrogant and prideful. It is being submissive. It is being patient.[48] Humility is recognition of who we are in our relation to God. It is recognizing that we are nothing without grace-the unearned, unmerited favor of God manifested through salvation and His continued blessings.

Humility says:

---

[47] Matthew 6: 19-21 Amplified Bible
[48] www.freedictionary.com

HE IS OMNIPOTENT – I am powerless without Him! *I can do all things through Christ who strengthens me.*[49]

Humility says:

HE IS OMNISCIENT – I know not much apart from Him! *"For My thoughts are not your thoughts, nor are your ways My ways," declares the LORD. "For as the heavens are higher than the earth, so are My ways higher than your ways and My thoughts higher than your thoughts.*[50]

Humility says:

HE IS OMNIPRESENT – I am only one person. I cannot be everywhere at one time. I can only be where I am right now. *I can never be lost to your Spirit! I can never get away from my God!* [8]*If I go up to heaven, you are there; if I go down to the place of the dead, you are there.* [9]*If I ride the morning winds to the farthest oceans,* [10]*even there your hand will guide me, your strength will support me.* [51]

Father, help us to trust in you and you alone. Help us to not fall victim to the pride of life. May it never ever be a motivating factor in our service for you. Help us to be truly Kingdom minded!

I like nice things. The Lord has blessed us to have a wonderful home, cars to drive, and income to sustain life, and yet I am reminded of Job. He and his family had it all and, he lost it all-- in a very short time! He became weak, but he did not turn his back on God. And in the end God restored back to him double for his trouble.

Father, help us to have the right attitude concerning things. Help us to have the right attitude concerning what has been given to us by you. Help us to hold nothing back from you. May our dependence be totally upon you. May you have all of our heart. Let it not be divided. May our treasure be found in you and you alone! Keep us from being snared by the pride of life.

---

[49] Philippians 4: 13
[50] Isaiah 55: 8-9 Amplified Bible
[51] Psalm 139: 7-10 Living Bible

STUDY QUESTIONS

1. Write down a detailed definition of the pride of life.

_____

_____

_____

_____

_____

_____

_____

2. Summarize 2 Corinthians 11: 22-33 in your own words.

_____

_____

_____

_____

_____

_____

_____

_____

_____

_____

3. When we are motivated by the pride of life; in what will we put our trust?

_____

_____

_____

_____

4. How do we gather, heap up and store treasures in heaven?

_____

_____

_____

_____

5. Define humility.

_____

_____

_____

_____

6. Humility says…

_____

_____

_____

_____

_____

_____

7. Read Job chapters 1 and 2. Record who, what, when, where and how concerning Job's life.

_____

_____

_____

_____

_____

_____

_____

_____

_____

8. What lessons can we learn from the life of Job as told in chapters one and two?

_____

_____

_____

_____

_____

_____

_____

_____

_____

_____

LOVE NOTES FROM THE FATHER

CHAPTER SEVEN
A Personal Love Story

"I knew you before you were formed within your mother's womb; before you were born I sanctified you and appointed you as my spokesman to the world." Jeremiah 1: 5 NLT

Everyone has a personal testimony. Everyone on the planet has a story to tell concerning the truth surrounding their parents, their birth, their childhood, right on up into adulthood. That does not mean that we will remember every little detail. Some will remember more than others, and some would rather not remember certain details; especially if those details were harmful. What I am about to share with you is my very own personal love story. Did I always feel loved? No. Was I always loved by those who were supposed to love me? Probably not. But, that is what we call life! It is living in a fallen world where things are not as God intended. However, the one thing that I have come to understand is that God loved me before I was even conceived, placed in my mother's womb, and that has been enough for me from the time I gave my heart to Him! So please understand, before you embark on this journey with me that I am not a victim! I have been violated in my life, and I have hurt others because of my pain, but this is not a re-telling whereby I bash those who harmed me. It is not a tell-all that I expose those who did me wrong! This is a journey of one of God's lovely ones whose steps He has ordered and loved through the pain. I blame no one except the enemy and take pleasure in the fact that I know what his end will be, because I have read the end of "THE BOOK" and we win!

I was born in an east-coast town, which at the time, was home to one of the world's largest military communities. My mom was only 17 years old when I was conceived and 18 when I was born. I was born in a Catholic Hospital which now I find quite interesting. I often wondered if those nuns prayed over me or for me. During my early childhood my biological father was not actively in my life, but that did not mean that I did not experience the love of a male figure at that time. I had my maternal grandfather, "Big Charlie." I loved "Big Charlie" and "Big Charlie" loved me! He was a longshoreman, but also a driver for one of the Fresh Fish Companies and would make pickups in North Carolina. He would take me along with him on some of the pickups and he always introduced me as his granddaughter. It always made me feel special to be known as "Charlie's granddaughter"! I guess it gave me a sense of belonging and affirmed me because my biological dad, for whatever reason, was not actively involved in my life. I grew up, in the beginning of my life living in a *shot-gun house* with an outhouse. At the time, I did not realize that we were considered poor. All I knew was that I was cared for, that I was loved.

In a few short years my mom and I moved out of that house. We moved into a community referred to as 'the projects," and my mom met a military man who would become my step dad. He was the one who took me to school on my first day. I remember feeling so proud with him holding my hand wearing my crinoline slip under my dress that made it poof out, white ankle socks and black patent leather shoes. And of course he had on his white navy uniform complete with the black kerchief tie and a Dixie cup hat.

In was in that community that I remember first hearing that God loved me. There was a lady named Miss Turner who would put out little chairs in her yard offering us kids Kool-Aid and cookies. Once we were engrossed in swilling down our drinks she would then tell us stories from the Bible. The seed of God's word was being planted in me at a very early age. That seed was further watered when I went to school. Mrs. Williams (my first and second grade teacher) would begin each school day with the Lord's Prayer, the pledge of allegiance to the flag and the 23rd Psalm. We would end the school day with *Numbers 6:24-26, ^{24} The Lord bless thee, and keep thee: ^{25} The Lord make his face shine upon thee, and be gracious unto thee:^{26} The Lord lift up his countenance upon thee, and give thee peace.* And this was in a public school! God loved me!

There was a Unity Lutheran church close to my school whose members looked nothing like me, but would come into our neighborhood and invite us to church. It was there that I remember seeing a filmstrip about the crucifixion, death and resurrection of Jesus Christ. I cannot tell you what I felt or testify of the impact that it had on my life at that time. All I know is that God loved me enough to send people my way to lead me to the truth!

It was my mom who taught me to say my prayers before I went to bed, *"Now I lay me down to sleep. I pray the Lord my soul to keep. If I should die before I wake. I pray the Lord my soul to take."* It was my mom who taught me to say grace before meals, *"God is great and God is good. Let us thank Him for our food. Bow our heads must all be fed. Give us Lord our daily bread. Amen."* God loved me!

I loved school and my mom tells me that I was an exceptional student. I loved my teachers and they seemed to take a liking to me. My fifth grade teacher even took me to church with her. She attended a Christian Methodist Episcopal Church (C.M.E.) and I remembered being baptized at that church. I was sprinkled and not immersed. Then at twelve years of age I attended a community Baptist church and it was there that I was baptized by being immersed in water. I will never forget the day as my mom was sitting in the back of the church. Up to this point in my life; I do not remember at any time repenting of my sins and giving my heart to the Lord. I just knew that I loved God and that He loved me.

My junior high and high school years were bitter-sweet. I was a good student, had some great friends, and others that turned out to not be friends at all. It was during this time in my life that I learned just how much being rejected could really pierce the heart. I fought within myself; like most tweens and teens do trying to find my place in life. I made a lot of good choices and I made a lot of bad ones too, that would haunt me for a very long time. God loved me!

Eventually, I made it through high school receiving my diploma 6 months later than my graduating class. I never got to march across that stage, and a month later I left all that was familiar for basic training in the United States Air Force. I was sent to Lackland Air Force Base in San Antonio, Texas. It was the first time that I had ever ridden on an airplane and the first time in my life that I had ventured that far away from home. My grandfather was also in the Air Force, and all concerned felt that it would be a good place for me. I was proud to be serving my country. I also learned that they would pay for me to obtain higher education. Prior to enlisting into the Air Force, I had enrolled in a vocational school with the goal to become a licensed practical nurse. I only made it through 6 months of a one-year program. It was not because I was not smart enough. I was doing quite well, actually. But, there was so much going on in my life at that time that it was better for me to just walk away, hoping that one day I would be able to start again. Have you ever had a dream snatched away from you and made you feel that you had completely failed? My dream was to be a nurse, and to not be able to finish the program was devastating. The poem by Langston Hughes, Dream Deferred comes to mind…

What happens to a dream deferred? Does it dry up
Like a raisin in the sun?

Or fester like a sore--
And then run?
Does it stink like rotten meat?
Or crust and sugar over--
like a syrupy sweet?

Maybe it just sags
like a heavy load.

Or does it explode?

God loved me!

During the next few years I would become an Airman in the United States Air Force. I would marry, have a beautiful baby girl, and end up getting a divorce; running away from a very abusive relationship. I contacted a very strange disease whose treatment for it was even worse than the symptoms of the disease. I would go through depression so severe that I did not want to live anymore. How could I possibly survive another BIG failure in my life! The rejection was too much to bear and yet, God loved me? How could He love me, and allow my heart to be broken. How could He comfort the pain? I was supposed to be in a better place by now. I had a daughter to support. I wanted to go to college and finish, and here I am with another failure under my belt; trying to recover from yet another very serious disease. I had lost everything! Did God really still love me?

For the next few years I became someone that I did not even know. I lived faster and harder than I ever had in my life. I did so many things that I am not proud of; some of them too shameful to even tell. And then it happened. I got into a very bad car accident. The accident happened very early in the morning as I was returning to work after running an errand. Because of the disease I was not sleeping at night, and refused to take the sleeping pills that the doctor had prescribed. I had always been afraid of getting hooked on drugs, so I was always cautious as to what I ingested. I fell asleep at the wheel. God loved me! It was a single car accident. Thank God, I did not hit anyone else. I slammed into the guard rail as I was exiting the highway. The accident happened right in front of the Mexican Baptist Children's Home (an orphanage). They were able to bring towels to help bring the bleeding of my injuries under control. There was a registered nurse in the car behind me who stopped and offered assistance. The accident happened just five minutes from the largest Air Force hospital in the United States at that time. But even before they came to help; when I was in that car I heard in my mind over and over again the 23rd Psalm. And then I heard a voice that called me by my name and somehow I knew that it was the voice of the One who loved me still. He said, "Vera turn off the car before it blows up." I reached for the ignition and turned off the engine, and put on the emergency brake. It was only then that I felt the pain from my injuries. For days I did not want to look at myself in the mirror as I could feel how swollen my face was. I had lost my two front teeth and had multiple fractures in my face from hitting the steering wheel. Thank God I had on my seat belt. I had a puncture wound in my leg whereby the leg should have been broken, but it was not. God loved me still!

Needless to say my car was totaled, and when I got the chance I went to the junk yard to see it. All I could do was gasp. I was told that there was no way that I should have come through that accident alive. Today I have a scar under my bottom lip and one above my top lip. I have a 2-inch scar on my left leg. The scars remind me that God loved me even when I did not love myself and protected me when the enemy wanted to take my life. God had a plan and a purpose for my life, and would do what needed to be done so that I would live out all my days. God loved me!

Within a few months I met the man who would become the love of my life. And before too long we married and had a son. He accepted my daughter as his own. He was a soldier in the United States Army. The first time that I saw him we were in church. He was sitting in the pew in front of me and my daughter touched him on his back, and he turned around. I apologized for her. Mike and I both were religious people. Even if we had gone out and partied on Saturday night we both knew enough to get up and go to church on Sunday morning. And then it happened! I received orders to Okinawa, Japan and he had orders to Fort Clayton, Panama. I will never forget the day that I stood in our little apartment and for the first time in many years I earnestly prayed, "God, I know that you are real and if you will keep me and my family together; I will serve you for the rest of my life." I went to work the next day and they told me to go over to the hospital squadron and ask for Senior Master Sergeant Hicks. When I got to the command section he was coming down the hall and I walked up to him and said, "Sir I know that you probably don't remember me…" and before I could finish my sentence he said, "Hi Vera it's been a while." You see I had served under him at a previous duty station. Within a few short months my husband and our children left on official orders for Misawa Air Base Japan. We left Texas on the same day, and on the same plane. God heard me. God answered me. God loved me!

For the next three years I served the Lord by attending the Gospel service in the military chapel. I knew nothing about discipleship. I knew nothing about being mentored. I served Him the best I could. I was still both green and rather rough around the edges. I applied myself at work and taking college courses. It was tough trying to juggle marriage, raising the kids, being faithful in church, and going to school. But I thank God for those days in Misawa. The community there was like family, and we made friendships there that still exist today. And then it happened! I was put in charge of the Environmental Medicine Section, and my responsibility was to track the interviewing, and treatment of all individuals who had contracted venereal diseases. A lot of our cases could be traced back to the Philippines and I would have to make telephone calls on a regular basis to an Airman there. One day she asked me seemingly, out of the blue, if I was a Christian. Of course I told her yes I was. And then she asked me if I was Spirit filled. I told her yes, because He lived on the inside of me. She chuckled and said okay. But after that conversation with her I could not shake what I was feeling inside. I was so uncertain, but pride would not let me ask anyone in my church family. God loved me.

We only had a few months left on our tour of duty, and the Chaplain (Chaplain Campbell) would go on quite a few temporary duty assignments to other places. During those times of his absence there was a Church of God Ministry to the Military preacher who would come and minister in his stead. It would astonish me how I would read something in the Bible during the week and he would either preach using the same passages of Scripture or God would use him to answer questions that I had on my mind while reading the word. God loved me!

Then it happened! Mike and I got orders. They were sending him to Fort Hood, Texas and me to Sheppard Air Force Base in Wichita Falls, Texas. This meant that we would now be a five-hour drive apart. The first day that I reported for duty I was introduced to the Airman that would be working for me. Her name was Airmen Linda Nelson. God had sent her from the Philippines and me from Japan, and there we were face to face. She attended the Maurine Street Church of God and that week invited me to go to a James Robison Crusade at the Bell Auditorium. I went with her. It was November 1984, and it was that night that I surrounded my heart completely to the Lord and I have never looked back. I begin going to her church. Pastor James and Sister Mildred Hill welcomed us with open arms. It was a time when African Americans were not welcomed in some churches in the south. There were people who did not take kindly to us being there. But Pastor Hill loved us, and he and his wife nurtured us and he stood up for us. He taught us how to love by loving us. Within a few months my husband gave his heart to the Lord and so did our daughter who was eight years old and they were baptized on the same night. God loved me!

For almost a year Mike would drive from Fort Hood on Friday evening arriving home at 10 pm and leave Sunday evening at 5 pm, to go back. I remember like it was yesterday how the children would cry so, because their dad had to leave us. God brought some wonderful mentors into our lives; Calvin and his wife Shonna. I remember her teaching me about prayer and fasting. It was during this time that God began to deal with me about the relationship with my husband and my children. You see my desire was to absolutely spend twenty years in the air force and then retire. I was more than at the half way mark. Then it happened. After fasting and praying I went to Shonna crying my eyes out, and told her that I felt that the Lord was leading me to transition out of the military, but how could I? I had just re-enlisted for four more years. All she said was, "Let's pray." Soon thereafter I sat down and wrote a letter to my commander requesting to be released from my commitment as I could no longer give the Air Force first priority in my life. I told him that I needed to be released in order to make my family the priority. They sent the children and I to the mental health folks to see if I qualified for a hardship discharge: I was turned down. I went back to my commander and he decided to send it up the Chain of Command anyway. There was a lady in our church who was the secretary for the officer that had the power to either approve it or disapprove it. When my paperwork came across her desk she called me and told me that she was going to lay hands on it and pray before taking it in, and I told her that I would also pray. I have no idea when she took it in or how much time passed. All I know is that when he brought the paperwork back out to her. He told her, "I spoke with Sgt. Warner and I assured her that her discharge would be approved." I tell you the truth; I never saw the man. He never spoke with me. As a matter of fact, my Honorable discharge does not have a signature on it to this day and yet I was issued my DD Form 214 that proves that I served, honorably, 11 years and 8 months. While on my way out of the Air Force I was told that I had earned enough credits for two associate degrees; one from the Community College of the Air Force and the other from the University of Maryland. God loved me!

It was hard leaving my brothers and sisters at the Maurine Street Church of God. When we left Pastor Hill gave Mike and me a Strong's Concordance and a Matthew Henry commentary that we have used so much throughout the years that the pages are falling out. He saw something in us that we did not even see in ourselves back then. God loved me!

After arriving at Fort Hood, we would only be there a few months before getting orders for Hawaii and the four years that followed would prove to be some of the most important in our lives. It would be there that we would be trained beyond our expectations and have miraculous encounters with God and be used by God! It was there that the Lord called us to the ministry and we said yes! It was there that I earned a Bachelor's degree from Wayland Baptist University Hawaii Campus (I got to march this time) and formed relationships that have lasted all these years. God still loved me!

Since those days Mike and I have gone through many trials that have only served to make us effective for Kingdom work. We have lived and served in Massachusetts, and- worked and pastored in Europe for a total of 17 years. We have had our hearts so broken that at times it was hard to even breath. There were times that all we had to hold on to was each other and the Lord. And yet God has allowed me to complete a Master's degree and both of us received ordination credentials with Mike having been appointed as an Ordained Bishop in the Church of God. God loves me!

One day I thought back over my life and I remembered that dream deferred. That dream that I had of wanting so badly to become a nurse and I started talking to the Lord about it. I asked Him if I had missed it. Perhaps I should have gone back to school to complete my nursing degree. He told me to get out the dictionary and to look up the definition of a nurse. When I did, I read that a nurse was one who assisted the physician in helping people to get well. Then I heard the Father say to me, "Am I not the GREAT PHYSICIAN?" All I could do was weep! No I had not missed it at all. For His ways are not our ways! Not too bad for a little girl from the projects and the best is still yet to come. The rest of the story has yet to be written! Yes, indeed God loves me!

I told you when you first started reading that this was not a tell all nor an expose of those who had done me wrong. I am not a victim. I choose not to be a victim. I am a victor! My prayer is that something about my journey will encourage you to not give up nor give in, but to remain steadfast knowing that God has a plan and a purpose for your life and that He loves you more than you can even think or imagine! Now that ought to motivate you to serve with pure motives!

NOW IT'S TIME TO TELL YOUR STORY...

Make a time line of your life from the time you were born up to present day, pinpointing key events in your life. Write it two ways; first write down all that you remember and then re-write your story in view of the cross of Jesus Christ with the attitude that, "No matter what happened to me in my past, I choose not to be a victim but will forgive and live a victorious life. Write it being motivated by love and not by revenge. Once you have written both versions ask a trusted friend to read them both.

_____

_____

_____

_____

_____

_____

_____

_____

_____

_____

_____

_____

_____

_____

_____

_____

_____

ABOUT THE AUTHOR

Vera LeRay Warner is the daughter of a United States Navy veteran, the granddaughter of both United States Air Force and United States Coast Guard veterans and is married to a United States Army veteran. Having such a rich military ancestry instilled in her a sense of adventure at a very early age that caused her to develop an almost insatiable desire for reading. As a youngster she would take the city bus downtown to the public library and come home with an arm load of books and would have every one of them read before they were due to be turned back in. That sense of adventure would also lead her, upon graduation from high school, to enlist in the United States Air Force and it was during her tour that lasted almost 12 years that she first began to write poems and short stories. Her creative writing led her to enroll in the Community College of the Air Force, and the University of Maryland where she earned Associate degrees at both. Vera later attended Wayland Baptist University (Hawaii Campus) and eventually earned her Bachelors in Christian Education and later went back to school and earned her Masters in Theology.

There were many twists and turns in her life but her greatest accomplishment was November 1984 when she surrendered her heart to the Lord Jesus Christ and became a Christian. It was also during 1984 that she was selected and listed in "Outstanding Young Women in America." From that time onward she went back to her writing but it was not until 2000 that her first literary work was published: CREATIVELY REAPING THE HARVEST: USING THE TEA AS AN OUTREACH MINISTRY. Vera has since authored EMBRACING THE LOVE OF THE FATHER, CULTIVATE MY HEART and THE MAKING. She was also a contributing author for SPEAK TO ME LORD INSPIRATIONAL WRITINGS BY WOMEN FOR WOMEN VOLUME 1. Her bible study books are currently being used for small group studies in the United States, the United Kingdom and Germany.

Vera currently serves as Founder and President of In His Image: Women of Excellence an international Spirit-led ministry whose mission is to encourage women to seek God as the primary source for healing and wholeness and to empower them to become so effective in "Kingdom" work that they will have an impact upon the world.

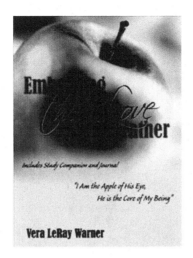

He is the core of my being!

Embracing the Love of the Father is a call to people everywhere, but especially to those who, for whatever reason, have not allowed themselves to be truly loved by the Father. This book is a reminder that He loves us so much and desires that we not just recognize His love for us but that we accept it as truth and embrace it with everything within us. This book re-emphasizes that we are "spiritual Israel". Therefore, we are the "apple of His eye", but most importantly, He is the "core" of our being.

"*Embracing the Love of the Father*" gives the very important foundation about the true Love of God in our searching we allow Him to establish a unique and everlasting personal love relationship. While studying the book and the scriptures, as well as working on your personal answers and inviting God to speak to you; God will guide you to a new level of faith and freedom (John 8:32) by revealing to you His truth and His Love.

Dr. Andreas and Gabriele Haun, Mühltal, Germany

I have read this book and studied from it as well. It is a great tool to uncover those problem areas that you may not even be aware of that need to be uncovered. *Embracing the Love of the Father* is so freeing and so personal that you cannot help but view yourself and how the Father loves you. This book will prove to be an invaluable investment into your life. Your life will be truly changed.

Andrea Johnson, United Kingdom

I Need a Heart fix!

The title of this study starts off with the word "cultivate" as does each of the chapter titles. "Cultivate" is a word used a lot in farming or agriculture and it means to prepare the land or the ground for use. It means to loosen or break up the soil. It further means to improve by labor, care or study. The heart is that ground that initially needs to be prepared by God to receive the seed of His Word.

Cultivate my Heart is a great resource that gives way for great discussion to take place if within a group setting and also deep reflection!

Samantha Roach United Kingdom

Glad I did this study after "Embracing the Love of the Father", because when He started cultivating I needed to remind myself that He was doing it in love. It is more like open-heart surgery; only you are fully awake. If you feel you need to go deeper with the Lord and bring forth much lasting fruit, then I strongly recommend this book.

Joyce Luutu, Author, United Kingdom

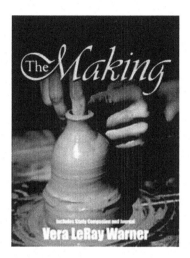

The Process

The Making is a window to be gazed into that will take the reader on a journey from birth, being born again, and revelation of the process that we all must go through to become effective servants in the Kingdom of God. It will cause the readers to examine their own lives in light of the expectations of the Father and to, prayerfully, get to the place whereby we willfully and joyfully allow the Holy Spirit to make us to fulfil our intended purpose, planned before we were even born!

SNEAK PEEK...

There is a term, "Self-Made Man" and it means having achieved success or recognition by one's own efforts. It means having made it by one's self (www.thefreedictionary.com). As saints of God, we know anything we have done or will do that is considered successful or good is not done through our own power and strength. It is because of the grace of God working within us and through us. We are women being made or fashioned by the hand of the Father and it is an ongoing process. And how does He make us? He does it through the trials that He allows in our lives. Now back to the text from a different translation: Consider it a sheer gift, friends, when tests and challenges come at you from all sides. You know that under pressure, your faith-life is forced into the open and shows its true colors. So don't try to get out of anything prematurely. Let it do its work so that you become mature and well-developed, not deficient in any way (James 1: 2-4 The Message Bible).

CONNECT WITH AUTHOR VERA LERAY WARNER

Friend me on Facebook: https://www.facebook.com/embracingHislove/

Twitter: https://twitter.com/veraleray

Subscribe to my blog: http://www.veraleraywarner.com/veras-blog/index.html

Visit my website: http://www.veraleraywarner.com/

Made in the USA
Columbia, SC
09 April 2018